McCLELLAN AND FREMONT:

A REPLY TO

"FREMONT AND McCLELLAN.

THEIR

POLITICAL AND MILITARY CAREERS REVIEWED."

BY ANTIETAM.

Audi alteram partem.

NEW YORK:
SINCLAIR TOUSEY, WHOLESALE AGENT, 121 NASSAU STREET.

Price, 10 Cents.

McCLELLAN AND FREMONT:

A REPLY TO

"FREMONT AND McCLELLAN,

THEIR

POLITICAL AND MILITARY CAREERS REVIEWED."

BY ANTIETAM.

Audi alteram partem.

NEW YORK:
SINCLAIR TOUSEY, WHOLESALE AGENT, 121 NASSAU STREET.

Price, 10 Cents.

WYNKOOP, HALLENBECK & THOMAS, PRINTERS,
No. 113 Fulton street, New York.

A MR. DENSLOW has written a pamphlet with this title: "Fremont and McClellan, Their Political and Military Careers Reviewed." It is the purpose of the following pages to point out some of the reviewer's inaccuracies and unfair statements, and to call his attention to some facts of history which he ignores.

The third sentence of Mr. Denslow's first page prompts us, at the start, to ask him whether he really thinks "there is no difference and no conflict as to the merits of McDowell and Pope?"

At the time this pamphlet was published, the former had already lost the confidence of the public and the army by his conduct at Bull Run, and forfeited that of a large portion of the country by his apparently *voluntary* inaction at Fredericksburgh. The latter had already marred the reputation gained at Island No. 10, by the gasconade of capturing "10,000" rebels below Corinth (who proved to be "men in buckram"), and disgusted all sensible men by his high-sounding bulletins from Washington—Alas, for the result! "How great a fall was there, my countrymen!"

Mr. Denslow opens his argument with an assumption for which there is no warrant. "Those who are satisfied with Fremont are generally those who voted for Lincoln, while the admirers of McClellan are those who voted for Breckinridge, Douglas, and Bell." Mr. Denslow is mistaken. His vision is distorted. He evidently does not see how some things have changed since '56 and '60. Those who admire Fremont are a minority of those who voted for Lincoln. They are confined almost exclusively to the readers of the *Tribune* and *Post*. What becomes of the *Commercial Advertiser, Times, and World?*—all newspapers representing the supporters of Lincoln. The zeal of the *Commercial Advertiser* in favor of McClellan is notorious. The *Times* has been strenuously, and is now virtually, a McClellan paper. The *World* is even more vigorous than the *Commercial Advertiser* in his support.

Outside of New York, we must reckon the *Albany Evening Journal* for Western New York, the *Springfield Republican* and the *Newburyport Herald* for New England—all supporters of Lincoln in '60—as among the admirers of McClellan. The same is true of other sections of the country. It thus becomes quite apparent that the sentiment in favor of McClellan is not confined to the supporters of Douglas, Breckinridge, and Bell. Add, that since the disastrous defeat of Pope, whose scorn of "lines of retreat" did not prevent him from seeking safety behind McClellan's intrenchments at Washington, the feeling in all parts of the country has been daily growing stronger and stronger in favor of McClellan as a good general, and what ground is there possibly left for Mr. Denslow's sweeping classification! *Ex pede Herclem.* This being the initial step of Mr. Denslow's "Review," we are not unprepared to note a lack of discernment (not to say lack of candor), throughout the entire pamphlet.

Mr. Denslow proceeds next to run a parallel between McClellan and Fremont, in respect of their birth and education, with the undisguised intent to show that McClellan is so strongly Southern in his ideas and associations that he cannot fairly be entitled to the good favor of his fellow-countrymen north of Mason and Dixon's line. This part of the "Review" —full of insinuations and manifesting a malice prepense—confirms the suspicion of want of candor which the opening page suggests. We are henceforth prepared to wonder at nothing. We cite a few extracts from this portion of the "Review," to show the animus of the writer:

"It is doubtless unimportant that the Southern press claim that McClellan, while at West Point, conspicuously preferred the society of Southern cadets to that of the Northern 'mud-sills,' in that institution."

"Indeed, Capt. McClellan was openly stated by the press, at the time, to have been one of the minor officers who, with Beauregard, Duncan, Mansfield Lovell, G. W. Smith, and others now in the rebel army, were to command in Quitman's intended fillibustering expedition against Cuba, which was broken up by Secretary Marcy. And, for his complicity with these movements for strengthening that slave power which is now the secession power, he was promoted from his brevet to a full captaincy by Jefferson Davis, and sent to the Crimea."

Now, in the name of loyalty and patriotism, to what purpose is all this? Granting, moreover, the facts all true, what evidence has Mr. Denslow that Capt. McClellan was in the secret of Davis and Quitman? As an officer in the army of the United States, he was bound to obey the orders of the War Department.

Better had it been for Mr. Denslow's favorite, Fremont, and better for the country, had Fremont imitated McClellan's example of obedience and subordination. Why cannot Mr. Denslow rather see cause for rejoicing that McClellan's prompt obedience, as his former good conduct on the battle-fields of Mexico, had so recommended him to the War Department that he was selected as one of a military commission to visit the Crimea and study the movements of large armies there—thus the better fitting him to command the armies of the Union! On the contrary, Mr. Denslow is in a petulant mood because Fremont had never such a school of instruction, and instead of rejoicing that the wicked schemes of Davis in the matter of Cuba left no stain upon the record of our gallant General, he unfairly insinuates that McClellan was concerned in those schemes. Instead of rejoicing that the mad ambition of the Southern leader was overruled for the especial good of McClellan, in qualifying him to be a commander of large armies, and so for the especial good of our country, Mr. Denslow the rather finds fault because McClellan has not proved a traitor, and left the field clear for Fremont. All this may be cunning, but it is not candid; it is not fair political criticism—it is the muttered growl of fanaticism foiled.

The mire is yet a little deeper, when we come to Mr. Denslow's next criticism of McClellan's political action. He does not like it, because the General of the Ohio department announced to the loyal people of Western Virginia that he would crush "with an iron hand" every attempt at slave insurrection. Considering the conspicuous fact of the loyalty of Western Virginia, and McClellan's thorough success in cleaning out the rebels from that entire region, we might wonder that Mr. Denslow is dissatisfied, were we not clearly convinced, from the whole tone of his "Review," that McClellan's dislike of radicalism causes Mr. Denslow's dislike of McClellan. Accordingly, our "reviewer" ventures on the following assertion: "Nay, it is not now to be doubted that any general insurrection among the slaves at that time, while it would have been far less sanguinary than the scenes which have since occurred in our efforts to preserve the Union, would have spread consternation among the rebels, and would have so divided and crippled their resources as to have speedily insured the triumph of the Union cause."

In contrast with this successful policy of McClellan in his department, we are invited to laud the contempt for the Federal

Government manifested by Fremont, in following "the precedent of the greatest Roman generals in ancient times, and of such generals as Jackson, Taylor, and Gaines in our own country," by assuming an authority to declare "the slaves of rebels free."

This brings us to the close of the review of Fremont and McClellan, politically considered.

Now, the pertinent inquiry arises—what, under the sun, has McClellan's political bias to do with his military efficiency? Will Mr. Denslow question the patriotism or efficiency of Butler? Yet, Butler voted for Breckinridge; nay, he was the President of the Charleston Convention, which nominated Breckinridge. Why, then, take such pains to show that McClellan is not Republican, as parties go? Are none but Republicans worthy to command the army of the Republic? Ask the thousands who compose that army.

We protest against this constant and continued attempt to foist the party issues of the past upon a country struggling, with the combined strength of loyal men of all parties, to put down this gigantic rebellion. Let Mr. Denslow, and his more prominent associates in this business, lend a helping hand toward sustaining the generals in the field, and not any longer, by sly hits and malicious insinuations at home, strengthen the rebel cause by weakening the unity of the people, who still stand strong for the Union.

Mr. Denslow's discussion of the respective military careers of Fremont and McClellan is marked by the same ill-concealed jealousy of the latter and the same extravagant and ill-timed laudation of the former which pervade the exclusively political pages of his pamphlet.

Having alluded in terms of just praise, which we, at least, have no desire to detract from, to Fremont's Rocky Mountain explorations, the "reviewer," with an ill grace, that is amusing, immediately brings forward, by way of contrast, we suppose, the unusual success of McClellan in the Mexican war. He seems to think it a hardship that Fremont, already a ten years' graduate, should be so nearly equaled in rank by McClellan, just from West Point; and he thus puts his spite in words: "At the close of the Mexican war, McClellan was even nearer to Fremont in rank than in reputation." Perhaps, had Fremont borne himself with the same commendable subordination that has always graced the military career of McClellan, even he might have got honor from the Mexican war.

We fail to perceive, with Mr. Denslow, the peculiar adaptedness of Fremont's Rocky Mountain explorations to his military experience. Crossing "great mountains and deserts," with only "twenty-five men," is, doubtless, a very bold adventure, though report has always perversely maintained that, but for Kit Carson, the bold Fremont would have lost his path quite as often as he found it. (His cognomen of "Pathfinder" seems, therefore, not altogether appropriate.)

But grant all that can be claimed for Fremont of honor on account of his explorations, grant that Humboldt praised him for his undoubted contributions to science, grant that as a "popular hero," by reason of all this romantic adventure, he received, likewise, "the applause of the people," still it remains to ask if these things indicate any peculiar fitness to command an army?

What germ of generalship does Mr. Denslow discover in them? On the contrary, his long sojourn in the mountains, where the necessities of the case made him absolute and uncontrolled, seems to have developed in Fremont that spirit of insubordination which is the prominent blemish in his character, and which doubtless is part of his South Carolina birthright. For we find him in the Mexican war getting into difficulty with his superior officers, and coming out of the difficulty with a blot upon his record. It is worthy of remark that the same haughty and insubordinate spirit has made itself conspicuous in all of Fremont's subsequent career.

Mr. Denslow's defense of his hero's California insubordination is very meagre. The evidence of General Kearney's asking pardon of Fremont is wanting. Commodore Stockton's known antipathy to Fremont gives no color to Mr. Denslow's statement of the relation between the Commodore and the insubordinate. The sentence of dismissal of the Court-martial is an unfortunate thing for Fremont.

In connection with this portion of his "Review," Mr. Denslow makes the following apology for his hero:

"The charge, nay, often the offense of insubordination being a frequent fact in the lives of the greatest military men, and occurring almost invariably when a far-seeing captain is called upon to sacrifice the interests of his command, or his country, to the caprice or ignorance of an official superior officer, allies him with such names as Cæsar, Bonaparte, Wellington, Wolfe, Jackson, and Scott, rather than furnishes evidence of military incompetency."

The alliance of Fremont's name with the names of Bonaparte and Wellington must seem peculiarly congruous to the people of this country, who have so lately had occasion to witness the military efficiency of Fremont, and his entire self-denying patriotism in all the phases of this war!

Mr. Denslow follows the blind guidance of a restless faction, in seeking every opportunity to ridicule West Point. It is "the envy of red-tape West Pointists," to whose dullness Fremont's "foresight was insubordination," that caused Fremont to be court-martialed.

Now, this persistent slurring of West Point is, in the last degree, prejudicial. Editors and "reviewers" are accustoming the people to a sort of flippant criticism, which, in the elder day, would have provoked summary punishment. West Point is, to-day, the bulwark of the nation. It is the supremest folly for men to suppose that war can be carried on regardless of all rule and all system.

West Point is the military school of the nation. The first essential of a soldier's duty is obedience, thorough, unhesitating obedience, to his superior officer. Insubordination is mutiny, and strikes at the root of discipline, without which there can be no army.

Why, then, declaim against the "red-tape" of West Point, which watches jealously the first symptoms of military incompetence! We have had some slight experience of the management of war by civilians. Our enemy trusts nothing to civilians; he manages his army through the educated science of West Point. *Fas est ab hoste doceri.*

Fremont's spirit of insubordination is to-day a disgrace to our army, because he is retained in commission after repeated acts of disobedience. It is, likewise, a disgrace to the nation's patriotism that he holds his commission after the paltry conduct of his resignation when Pope was called East. The American people may well fear for the result, if this embryo despot should ever be put in command of the army. Whenever and wherever Fremont has come under the questioning eye of impartial criticism, he has been found wanting. Dismissed from the army by sentence of court-martial, for insubordination and disobedience, he has lately incurred the most sweeping censures from the Committee appointed to investigate his conduct of affairs in Missouri. Of that Committee, no less a man than Judge Holt, of Kentucky, was Chairman—a man whose patriotism is unquestioned, and whose candor is equal to his patriotism. And now Fremont caps the climax of his career by resigning his command at the most critical juncture, thus depriving the nation of that magnificent generalship which his friends claim to belong to him. Is this evidence of patriotism?

We have dwelt at large upon this branch of Mr. Denslow's pamphlet, in order to expose the sophistries that seek to bring West Point in question before the people, and to elevate, in place of a well-educated system of scientific warfare, the dangerous insubordinations of haughty civilians, and the rash manœuvres of generals who move an unsupported brigade to oppose a *corps d'armée*.

Mr. Denslow's next step is to complain, in a most melancholy way, because McClellan having resigned from the army ("owing, it is said, to the fact," Mr. Denslow, with singular and evidently unalloyed regard for truth, informs us, "that his limited prospects in his profession as a soldier stood in the way of his marriage"—surely there is no base motive in this, nor, therefore, any particular reason to violate the proprieties of controversy, not less than the delicacies of social etiquette, by introducing the statement)—Mr. Denslow, we say, proceeds to complain, because McClellan, having resigned from the army, is, on the breaking out of the war, commissioned as a Major-General of Volunteers by Governor Dennison, of Ohio, while Fremont, who has been dismissed the service, must needs await the action of a partisan Congress before he can receive the commission which the people in no single State of the Union would have supported their Governor in granting him. This is distasteful to Mr. Denslow, but such, nevertheless, is the fact, and so our generous and candid "reviewer" classes McClellan with Patterson, and tells us, we must not be surprised if "men occasionally win rank as courtiers which they had not won as soldiers" (a remark which is doubtless just, and may with emphasis be applied to John C. Fremont), and adds, that "no one supposes" (that is, Mr. Denslow does not suppose) "that had McClellan not resigned from the regular army, he would at this moment, without being under fire upon any battle-field, have risen to a higher rank than all his three senior officers." In what respect will this remark not equally apply to Fremont? Rather, why will it not with more accuracy apply to Fremont? For Mr. Denslow has himself already told us that McClellan "had won creditable mention as a lieutenant of engineers" in Mexico, and every one who is familiar with the history of the Mexican war knows how the gallant lieutenant distinguished himself in several battles. Yet, Mr. Denslow says, McClellan was never "under fire upon any battle-field." Fie, Mr. Denslow! McClellan, however, Mr. Denslow himself being historian, had had opportunities not accorded to Fremont, of observing the movements of large armies in Europe, at the Crimea. But this, instead of being any recommendation to McClellan, in the eyes of our "reviewer," is a fault, for the reason that Fremont had never any such opportunity.

To follow Mr. Denslow through the mass of blunders and stupidities with which he seeks to dispraise McClellan, would be a task of the reader's patience hardly worth the while, for any candid reader must himself easily perceive the glaring inconsistencies of the military portion of the pamphlet. Some perversions of facts, however, may be noted, and some unfair inferences refuted.

Mr. Denslow lays great stress upon the fact that "McClellan was not personally present in any of the battles in Western Virginia." What would our sage critic thence infer? Apparently nothing, for he immediately adds that "the credit of being the commander of the department in which the battles were fought justly belongs to McClellan." That is to say, McClellan, as commander of that department, is justly entitled to the glory of having, by the plan and strategy of his campaign, quite cleared the Kanawha valley of the rebels. Yet, Mr. Denslow is not satisfied till he has shown that McClellan was prevented from engaging the enemy in battle, at Rich Mountain, by his own strategy, in compelling them to evacuate their position. Mr. Denslow sees no evidence of generalship in this. His idea of a general seems to be the impression got when a child, from the highly-colored engravings of a furious charge, led by one personage, conspicuous among the rest, on a coal-black charger.

Mr. Denslow needs to be informed that, as the world pro

gresses, the art military becomes more and more a game of skill, like chess, rather than the onset of furious legions, like the fierce fights of the Crusades. Perhaps Pope's brilliant campaign in Virginia has already taught Mr. Denslow something of this.

Our comprehensive and sagacious "reviewer" proceeds in the next place to give us a new theory of our first defeat at Bull Run, namely, that "though McDowell and his troops fought far better than any general or troops in Western Virginia," (he, of course, excludes McClellan, who, he considers, had done no fighting there), Scott lost us the day at Bull Run. In the light of McDowell and Pope's second battle of Bull Run, Mr. Denslow's theory is very easily understood.

Next follows the second chapter of the jeremiad over the appointment of McClellan by Governor Dennison, "an appointment," Mr. Denslow exclaims in grief, not in anger, "which made him the only major-general (though of three months' volunteers), except Scott, then in the service." Alas for Fremont! the Rocky Mountain hero of only "twenty-five men!"

Mr. Denslow needs to be reminded, just at this point of his argument, in connection with his disgust at the appointment of McClellan, after the defeat of Bull Run, how, as by intuition, all eyes were, at that critical juncture, turned to the chieftain who had won the first real successes of the war. His malignant enemies may jeer at McClellan for his want of dash since he took command of a large army that needed to be handled with great caution, because in the presence of a larger army commanded by skillful officers. But surely the campaign of Western Virginia had been as rapid and as brilliant as the most impatient could desire. There was no difference in McClellan after he assumed command at Washington, but he had now a different field of operations, and different officers to oppose. The secret of McClellan's success lies in this, that he takes things as he finds them. The dash and *élan* that might succeed in the mountain passes of the Kanawha would not avail on the plains of Manassas.

The nation has tried twice to accomplish what McClellan seems always to have considered impossible, and with what result? Ask that army, which first McDowell, and afterwards Pope, with such high pretensions, led forth to inglorious defeat. Mr. Denslow may forget the splendid new order of things inaugurated at Washington after McClellan took command, but the country will not.

Our "reviewer" now proceeds to contrast with the foregoing inglorious conduct of McClellan the brilliant campaign of Fremont in Missouri. We have not the space to go into a detailed narrative of the facts concerning Fremont's career at the West. Nor is there need. The whole question is set at rest by the full and lucid report of the Committee appointed for the express purpose of looking into the conduct of affairs in Missouri under Fremont. That Committee, headed by Judge Holt, of Kentucky, than whom the purity and exalted patriotism of no man's character are more conspicuous, found a heavy verdict against Fremont. They had all the facts before them, and their impartiality is unquestioned. We know well, from the contemporaneous record of the newspapers, how inaccessible Major-General John Charles Fremont made himself; how he surrounded himself with more than regal state; how colonels and captains and civil officers, charged with important dispatches, were made to stand, like Henry V. at the door of his Holiness the Pope, doing seeming penance for their audacity in seeking to address his Excellency the General. It is probable that by this means Fremont lost more regiments than would have sufficed to reinforce both his own and the army of the East.

But, says Mr. Denslow, "Fremont had long been accustomed to prominent command." Delicate and high-souled Fremont! Unworthy "boot-jack mud of Missouri!" Stupid people of Missouri, entertaining "an angel unawares!"

But Mr. Denslow's statement is a sweeping one, when he lays the responsibility of Lyon's defeat upon McClellan. Further on, in the course of his pamphlet, our "reviewer" speaks of the victories in the West, "in the departments which McClellan did *not* command." Will Mr. Denslow inform us which is which?

We deny altogether, however, this statement of the pamphleteer: "One point is proven. The strategy which compelled the surrender of Mulligan originated at Washington, not at St. Louis." Where may one find this proof?

We are informed in this connection, by Mr. Denslow, of one occasion when Fremont obeyed orders. Let us thank him for finding this sole instance. The Administration sends to Fremont for certain regiments. Fremont is just ready to send those very regiments to the aid of Mulligan, and remonstrates. The Administration repeats the order. Fremont yields. Whereupon, in emphatic capitals, Mr. Denslow declares that "FREMONT OUGHT TO HAVE DISOBEYED THE ORDER."

Unfortunately for the "reviewer's" argument, he has already told us that "Sturgis and others had been ordered to the relief" of Mulligan. Now, we know that Sturgis received his orders too late, although a long march nearer Mulligan than Fremont's St. Louis regiments, and only arrived in time to hear of the surrender. Sturgis was strong enough alone, *if ordered in time*, to reinforce Mulligan. It won't do, Mr. Denslow. Fremont is known to have disregarded the first dispatches of Mulligan. He only ordered Sturgis at the last moment, and then it was too late. So that to say that those St. Louis regiments being ordered to Washington was the cause of Mulligan's surrender is all moonshine.

The story has been told that one of the officers dispatched on a special mission to Major-General John Charles Fremont, to inform him of Mulligan's dangerous and exposed position, "danced attendance" (to use the officer's own language) on his excellency and his haughty aids for several days, without gaining admittance to the sacred presence, and finally returned in disgust to Lexington, to share the fate of his comrades.

Mr. Denslow says: "It would be in vain for us to attempt to do justice to Fremont's hundred days in Missouri." We feel a like inadequacy. He found the State trembling in the balance between Secession and Union. He left it followed by the execration of Union men all through the State. This is what Mr. Denslow means probably by saying "he left it Union."

We beg leave to ask Mr. Denslow again for the proof, when he tells us that "it is known" (this very ambiguous expression is a favorite with our "reviewer," but unhappily it has not the sanction by any power, though somewhat the same style, of the authoritative phrase—"It is written")—"it is known" that the "entire plan" of the western campaign was Fremont's. Who knows it?

Mr. Denslow exclaims at last in triumph: "But Fremont's chief offense consisted in having spoken 'FREEDOM TO THE SLAVES OF REBELS.'"

We beg leave to point out Mr. Denslow's error. Fremont's offense consisted in assuming an authority which the Government itself was not yet prepared to take. His offense was the same old story of insubordination. We are sorry that the facts of history prevent Fremont from being a martyr to his love of freedom.(!) That period is yet to come, and if it ever come, we may say with Hamlet: "Then is millennium come."

We are sorry, also, that the truth of history prevents our indorsement of Mr. Denslow's statement, that "Fremont's vigorous anti-slavery policy was regarded by the loyal North with universal approbation."

It neither has been, nor is so regarded anywhere. Our "reviewer" introduces the usual sneer at the Border States, forgetful of their utter desolation, under the ravages of war, which the North knows nothing of, declares McClellan responsible for the removal of Fremont (how much more is to be attributed to McClellan!), and proceeds next to ridicule McClellan's reorganization of the army.

But our own patience fails us at this point. Nor is it necessary to follow Mr. Denslow in his further denunciation of McClellan, the rest of his pamphlet being devoted exclusively to that purpose.

The facts and figures, and the reasons, so far as consistent with public safety, of McClellan's six months at Washington, have been clearly stated and succinctly narrated in an editorial in the New York *World* of Aug. 7, since published in pamphlet form. We commend the perusal of it to Mr. Denslow.

Another pamphlet has lately appeared, under the title of "Major-General George B. McClellan, from Aug. 1st, 1861, to Aug. 1st, 1862," written by an army officer, which discusses, in a clear and intelligible manner, the conduct of military affairs under McClellan, and, while satisfactorily refuting the statements of Senator Chandler and his followers, establishes, beyond dispute, the military skill and splendid management of the Peninsular campaign. We recommend Mr. Denslow to a perusal of this also.

The "logic of events" has demonstrated the folly of that mistaken policy (called vigorous) to which the President, unfortunately no longer trusting military affairs in military hands, at last yielded assent, which moved the army fully a month before its time. The splendid victories of the West have all to be fought over again. The Virginia Department is as badly off as it was a year ago, and only the foresight of McClellan, who, a year ago, dug his intrenchments around Washington, saved the nation from the dire results of Pope's stupidity, on the occasion of the second grand Bull Run skedaddle.

Let Mr. Denslow note this important fact, that, in the only two expeditions that have been entirely free from political interference at Washington, the success of the Union arms has been and is complete. Those two expeditions were planned and ordered by Gen. McClellan, and executed by those gallant civilians, Butler and Burnside. What a pregnant comment is their rich success on the meddling fanaticism which has marred and wrecked the other plans of our brave commander!

Since Mr. Denslow's pamphlet was written, the Maryland campaign has put the stamp of pre-eminent efficiency on McClellan's military skill, and it is now seen that, when master of his movements and his men, he knows right well how to make himself master of his enemy. The facts leak out, also, that the failure to completely rout the rebels, after the battle of Antietam, is due to the disregard of McClellan's advice in the matter of Harper's Ferry—which point was not under his command, and the conduct of which he himself could not, therefore, control.

Yet, even now, with the grand successes of the last month fresh in our minds and hearts, and the whole nation exultant and rejoicing, the malignant influences that have operated against the hero of Antietam, ever since he had command, are again at work. The persistency with which some people decry McClellan is as though a conclave of owls should declare at noon-day that the sun did not shine.

We may safely trust to the verdict of history the reputation of a man who, in the midst of abuse, malignant and long continued and unsparing and uncrupulous, holds himself too proud to descend into the arena of partisan controversy, and fling the lie back into his traducers' teeth.

The magnificent reticence that can thus calmly await the sure final issue, confident and hopeful, is fit ally to that patriotism which has always yielded prompt obedience to superior orders—whether stripping its possessor of all command, or investing him with the supreme command. This is that patriotism that, rather than resign, made McClellan declare: "I am ready to shoulder my musket, and go into the ranks."

Contrast Fremont's wounded sense of honor with conduct like this! Fremont stands forth as the exponent of insubordinate radicalism, that scruples at nothing—in the vain pursuit of a chimera, never possible to be realized.

McClellan is tne representative of that respect for constitutional authority which secures the only freedom society ever acquires, and which is the chief boast and glory of the United States!

SEPTEMBER 30, 1862.

www.ingramcontent.com/pod-product-compliance
Lightning Source LLC
LaVergne TN
LVHW020635110826
845149LV00004B/1207

9781418191467